Step-by-Step Irish
An Irish Language Workbook for Beginners

James Joyce

do dhaideo

Copyright © 2020, 2017 James Joyce

All rights reserved.

ISBN: 1545350795
ISBN-13: 978-1545350799

LESSONS

1	Pronunciation	p. 6
2	Plurals and the Definite Article	p. 10
3	Pronouns	p. 13
4	Present Tense Verbs	p. 17
5	Adjectives and Questions	p. 22
6	Prepositions	p. 27
7	The Present Participle	p. 32
8	The Copula	p. 36
9	Past Tense Verbs	p. 40
10	The Imperative Mood	p. 45
11	Future Tense Verbs	p. 49
12	Common Phrases	p. 53

FOREWORD

Though modern-day Irish is nowhere near as prevalent as it was in the Ireland of old, the Irish language still serves as an integral part of Gaelic culture. Those in the Irish *Gaeltachtaí* still rely on the language for day-to-day communication, and many young Irishmen and Irishwomen take Irish language classes in school.

The Irish language is considered to be one of the hardest languages to pick up – not only is its vocabulary very complex, but grammatically speaking, Irish can be a nightmare to learn. However, with dedication and patience, learning Irish is certainly not an impossible task.

This workbook is presented in twelve lessons. Each lesson will feature a table of vocabulary (except for Lesson #1), an explanation of grammatical concepts, and activities to reinforce what has been learned. Answers to these activities can be found in the back of the workbook.

This workbook certainly does not cover all the ins and outs of the Irish language; however, it provides a great basis from which the tongue can be learned. Supplemental activities, such as Irish language TV shows and radio programs, are highly recommended.

It is my hope that this workbook will both teach you the basics of Irish and inspire you to continue studying the Irish language.

Sláinte!

James Joyce

·1·
PRONUNCIATION

The Irish alphabet

The Irish alphabet consists of eighteen letters, all of which are used in the English language. These letters are listed below.

a, b, c, d, e, f, g, h, i, l, m, n, o, p, r, s, t, u

Though the letters j, k, q, v, w, x, y, and z are not officially members of the Irish alphabet, they can be found in words borrowed or derived from other languages.

veidhlín → violin
vóta → vote
zú → zoo

The *fada*

In Irish, an accent mark is called a *fada* (pronounced fah-duh), which literally means *long*. When a fada is placed over a vowel, the pronunciation of this vowel changes. Below, these changes are shown using English words.

a	b<u>a</u>t	á	<u>aw</u>ful
e	b<u>e</u>t	é	pl<u>ay</u>
i	b<u>i</u>t	í	f<u>ee</u>t
o	b<u>o</u>t	ó	l<u>ow</u>
u	b<u>u</u>t	ú	fl<u>ew</u>

In addition, a fada can significantly change the meaning of a word.

>   briste → broken
>   brísté → pants
>   caca → excrement
>   cáca → cake

As my Grandad used to say, don't mix up your *caca* and your *cáca*.

Broad and slender

Much like vowels, there are two types of consonants in the Irish language: broad and slender. Broad consonants are always surrounded by the vowels a, o, and u, whereas slender consonants are surrounded by e and i.

The rule "broad with broad, slender with slender" means that consonants are *always* surrounded by vowels of the same category – you'll never see a consonant between a slender vowel and a broad vowel.

>   te → hot (the t is **slender**, as it is touching e)
>   fuar → cold (the f and r are **broad**, as they are touching u and a, respectively)
>   anocht → tonight (the n is **broad**, as it is between a and o)

In terms of pronunciation, broad consonants are typically pronounced the way they would be vocalized in English. Exceptions can be found in the letters d and t.

>   d → pronounced like the English letter d or like the word "the"
>   t → pronounced like the English letter t or like "th"

Slender consonants are a bit harder to pronounce. They can either be pronounced like their English counterparts or with a y-glide, meaning that a faint "y" sound is made after the consonant is vocalized. For example, in the word *beo* (alive), the b is slender. Hence, the word is pronounced *B-yeo*.

Exceptions to slender pronunciation are found in d, s, and t.

d → pronounced *dy* or *jy*
s → pronounced *sh* or *shy*
t → pronounced *ty* or *tchy*

No need to worry too much about the specifics of pronunciation yet, as each vocab word presented in this workbook comes with a pronunciation guide.

Lenition and eclipsis

The beginnings of Irish words can be changed by the preceding word. These changes are often seen as the most difficult parts of the Irish language; however, with practice, they will come naturally.

In lenition, an h is added after the first letter of words starting with the consonants listed below. This changes the pronunciation of the letter; these variations in pronunciation are explained in parentheses.

b → bh (*v* or *w*)   c → ch (*ch* as in lo*ch*)   d → dh (*y*)
f → fh (silent)   g → gh (*ch* as in lo*ch*)   m → mh (*w*)
p → ph (*f*)   s → sh (*h*)   t → th (*h-yah*)

Eclipsis involves adding a letter before the first letter of words starting with the consonants listed below. The pronunciation of these changes are much easier, as the eclipsis is simply pronounced instead of the original first letter. In other words, the original first letter becomes silent in the case of eclipsis.

b → mb   c → gc   d → nd   f → bhf (silent)
g → ng   p → bp   t → dt

Don't worry about when lenition are eclipsis are used, as this will be explained in later chapters. For now, just know that these changes exist and how each change affects each letter.

Word stress

In Irish, stress is typically placed on the first syllable of spoken words. However, in Munster Irish, a dialect spoken in the south of Ireland, stress is placed on the second or third syllable.

Pronunciation Review

→ Vowels without fadas are pronounced as they would be in English, but vowels with fadas have longer sounds.
→ Broad consonants are typically pronounced as they would be in English, with a few exceptions. Slender consonants have a y-glide, which adds a faint "y" sound after the consonant.
→ Lenition adds an "h" after the first letter of some words, while eclipsis adds an additional letter before the first letter.

Add lenition and eclipsis to the words below. If the word cannot be lenited or eclipsed, simply rewrite the original word.

		Lenition	Eclipsis
1)	forc	_____	_____
2)	spúnóg	_____	_____
3)	scian	_____	_____
4)	pláta	_____	_____
5)	cupán	_____	_____
6)	naipcín	_____	_____

Determine whether the underlined letter is broad or slender.

7)	forc	broad	slender
8)	spúnóg	broad	slender
9)	scian	broad	slender
10)	pláta	broad	slender
11)	cupán	broad	slender
12)	naipcín	broad	slender

· 2 ·
PLURALS AND THE DEFINITE ARTICLE

Vocabulary

IRISH SINGULAR		IRISH PLURAL		ENGLISH
an	/un/	na	/nuh/	the
arán	/a-rawn/			bread
bainne	/bahn-yay/			milk
bean	/bahn/	mná	/muh-naw/	woman
Béarla	/bear-lah/			English *(lang.)*
bialann *(f)*	/bee-a-luhn/	bialanna	/bee-a-luh-na/	restaurant
buachaill	/bwa-hull/	buachaillí	/bwa-hull-lee/	boy
cailín	/cah-leen/	cailíní	/cah-leen-nee/	girl
duine	/dih-nah/	daoine	/dee-nah/	person
Éire *(f)*	/ee-ray/			Ireland
fear	/fair/	fir	/fihr/	man
Gaeilge *(f)*	/gail-gay/			Irish *(lang.)*
Sasana	/sawsa-nuh/			England
scoil *(f)*	/skull/	scoileanna	/skull-una/	school
teach	/takk/	tithe	/tih-hih/	house
uisce	/ish-kay/			water
úll	/ool/	úlla	/oola/	apple

From this point on, each chapter will contain a vocabulary section. These new words will be used to help explain grammatical concepts. From left to right, each vocabulary table contains an Irish word, its phonetic pronunciation, the plural form of the word, the plural pronunciation, and the English translation.

The definite article

In English, there are three articles: **the**, which is the definite article, and **a/an**, which are indefinite articles. The Irish language differs in that there is no indefinite article; rather, there is only a definite article, which is expressed by the Irish word *an*, meaning "the."

> buachaill → boy or a boy
> an buachaill → the boy

Unlike English, the definite article changes when the following noun is in plural form. In this case, the word *na* is used instead of the singular *an*.

> na buachaillí → the boys

The definite article is also used in ways that differ from the term *the* in English. For example, the definite article is placed before the names of languages and countries.

> an Béarla → English (referring to language)
> an Sasana → England

Due to different noun cases, there are many other ways in which the Irish definite article is used; however, these conditions will be described in later lessons.

Noun gender

All Irish nouns are either masculine or feminine. Though determining Irish noun gender is not as easy as in Spanish or French, each vocabulary table in this book includes noun gender. Because a large majority of Irish nouns are masculine, only feminine nouns are noted through the use of an *(f)* next to the Irish word.

All feminine nouns beginning with consonants are **lenited** following the definite article, while masculine nouns beginning with consonants remain the same. However, a t is added to the beginning of most feminine nouns that start with the letter s.

an bainne → the milk

an b<u>h</u>ialann → the restaurant

Meanwhile, while feminine nouns beginning with vowels are unchanged by the definite article, most masculine nouns that start with vowels add t- to their beginning when following the definite article.

an t-arán → the bread

Plurals

Irish plurals are somewhat complicated in that not all nouns have the same plural ending. Though there are strategies by which the plural of an Irish noun can be determined, for now, it's easiest to simply memorize the plural form of each word.

Plurals and the Definite Article Review

→ Irish does not have an indefinite article, and the definite article is *an* when used with a singular noun and *na* when used with a plural noun.

→ After the definite article, feminine nouns beginning with consonants are lenited by adding an "h" and most masculine nouns that start with vowels have "t-" added to their beginnings.

Add the definite article to the words below. Then, translate each word into English.

		Definite Article	Translation
1)	fear	_____	_____
2)	uisce	_____	_____
3)	bialanna	_____	_____
4)	teach	_____	_____
5)	daoine	_____	_____
6)	Gaeilge	_____	_____
7)	cailíní	_____	_____
8)	mná	_____	_____

· 3 ·
PRONOUNS

Vocabulary

IRISH SINGULAR		IRISH PLURAL		ENGLISH
mé	/may/			I/me
tú	/too/	sibh	/shihv/	you
sé	/shay/			he/him
sí *(I)*	/shee/			she/her
muid	/moo-id/			we/us *(Conn.)*
sinn	/shin/			we/us
siad	/shee-ad/			they/them
féin	/hayn/			self

Word order

In English, sentences typically follow the SVO, or subject - verb - object, word order. The subject of the sentence, or the word to which the verb pertains, comes first. Next comes the verb, which is followed by the object, or the word to which the verb is being done. For example, in the sentence "You learn Irish," 'you' is the subject, 'learn' is the verb, and 'Irish' is the object.

In Irish, sentence structure is a bit different, as sentences follow a VSO word order. In this case, the verb comes first, followed by the subject and object. Thus, in Irish, the sentence "You learn Irish" would be structured as "Learn you Irish." Irish verbs will be covered in a later lesson.

Pronouns

When used as the subject of a sentence, Irish pronouns follow the forms shown in the vocabulary table. To demonstrate this, the Irish verb *feic* will be used in its present tense form.

    feic → see
    feiceann → see (*present tense*)

    Feiceann mé an bainne → I see the milk
    Feiceann sí na mná → She sees the women

The sentences shown above each follow the VSO word order, with *feiceann* - the verb - coming first. The subject of both sentences is a pronoun, with *bainne* and *mná* as objects.

However, when being used as the objects of a sentence, the pronouns *sé, sí,* and *siad* adopt different forms.

    é → he *(obj)*
    í → she *(obj)*
    iad → they *(obj)*

In effect, when the pronouns *sé, sí,* and *siad* are the objects of a sentence, they each drop their first letter. The other pronouns stay the same regardless of their use as a subject or object.

    Feiceann sí mé → She sees me
    Feiceann mé í → I see her
    Feiceann siad na fir → They see the men
    Feiceann na fir iad → The men see them

Note how she is *sí* in the first sentence, as it is the subject of the sentence, but is *í* in the second sentence, as it becomes the object. The same goes for they, which transforms from *siad* to *iad*.

Adding *féin*

In order to add emphasis to Irish pronouns, the word *féin*, meaning self, may be added directly after the pronoun. Though this does not change the meaning of the sentence, it adds emphasis to the afflicted pronoun. Using féin to demonstrate emphasis is very common among native Irish speakers.

tú → you
tú féin → yourself

Feiceann mé tú → I saw you
Feiceann mé tú féin → I saw yourself

The Irish political party *Sinn Féin*, meaning *Ourselves*, uses this technique.

Dialects

Much like how English words differ between the United States and Great Britain, different regions of Ireland can, at times, use separate words with the same meanings. Though most of Ireland uses *sinn* to express the pronoun "we," counties in the Connaught region of Ireland use the word *muid*.

Dialects will be discussed in depth in a later lesson. For now, a note will be made each time a dialectal difference is relevant to the lesson at hand.

Pronouns Review

- → Instead of the English SVO word order, a VSO word order is used in Irish, with the verb coming before the subject and object.
- → When being used as the subject of a sentence, the Irish pronouns *mé, tú, sé, sí, muid/sinn, sibh,* and *siad* are used.
- → As objects, *sé, sí,* and *siad* become *é, í,* and *iad*.
- → *Féin*, meaning self, can be added after pronouns to express emphasis.

Fill in the blanks using the appropriate Irish form of the pronoun in parentheses.

1) Feiceann _____ (me) na buachaillí.
2) Feiceann na fir _____ (her).
3) Feiceann _____ (he) an scoil.
4) Feiceann an bean _____ (us).
5) Feiceann _____ (you, *plural*) mé féin.
6) Feiceann an cailín _____ (them).
7) Feiceann _____ (her) an bhialann.
8) Feiceann na mná _____ (yourself).

·4·
PRESENT TENSE VERBS

Vocabulary

IRISH SINGULAR		IRISH PLURAL		ENGLISH
airgead	/ar-ih-gid/			money
ard	/ard/			tall
Bríd *(f)*	/breejd/			Bridget
cara	/car-uh/	cairde	/car-djay/	friend
dearg	/dare-ugg/			red
focal	/fuk-ull/	focail	/fok-ull/	word
Máire *(f)*	/moy-ra/			Mary
muintir *(f)*	/mween-cher/	muintireacha	/mween-cher-acka/	family
Séamus	/shay-mus/			James
Seán	/shawn/			John
abair	/ah-bear/			say
bí	/bee/			be
bris	/breesh/			break
déan	/dan/			do
faigh	/fay/			get
feic	/feck/			see
ithe	/ith/			eat
oibrigh	/ub-rig/			work
ól	/ull/			drink
téigh	/tay/			go
úsáid	/oo-say-id/			use

To be

In Irish, there are two present forms of "to be" - *tá* and *is*, both of which express the English word "is." In this section, we will focus on *tá*, which is the present tense form of the verb *bí*.

Tá is used when describing someone or something, while *is* is used when connecting two nouns or pronouns. For example, when translating the sentence the boy is tall, *tá* would be used, as "the boy" is being described. Meanwhile, in Irish, the sentence he is a boy would use *is*, as two pronouns - "he" and "boy" - are being compared.

    tá /taw/ → is *(present form of to be)*

Because of the VSO word order of most Irish sentences, *tá* is typically found in the beginning of the sentence.

    Tá an buachaill ard → The boy is tall
    Tá tú dearg → You are red

In the sentence above, *tá* (the verb) comes first, followed by the subject.

When *tá* is combined with the pronouns *mé* or *muid*, contractions - known as the synthetic form - can be created. *Tá* + *mé* becomes *táim*, and *tá* + *muid* becomes *táimid*.

    Tá mé ard → I am tall
    Táim ard → I am tall

While both of the forms shown above are acceptable, in spoken Irish, it is much easier to form contractions. As a dialectical note, in the Connaught region of Ireland, the synthetic form is much less common.

The present tense

In Irish, the present tense is formed by adding an ending to the root verb. The table at the beginning of this chapter shows these root forms, so in order to form the present tense, certain endings must be added.

Verb endings are determined through two factors: syllable count and broad/slender. Verbs with only one syllable fall under the "first conjugation" of present tense verbs. The table below shows the endings that must be added onto first conjugation verbs to form the present tense.

Pronoun	Broad Ending	Slender Ending
mé	-ann mé or -aim	-eann mé or -im
tú	-ann tú	-eann tú
sé	-ann sé	-eann sé
sí	-ann sí	-eann sí
muid	-ann muid or -aimid	-eann muid or -imid
sibh	-ann sibh	-eann sibh
siad	-ann siad	-eann siad

Depending on whether the last vowel in the verb is broad or slender, the endings above are added onto one-syllable verbs when forming the present tense. In addition, as we saw with the verb *tá*, contractions can be formed when the present tense is used with the pronouns *mé* and *muid*.

> ól → drink
> ólann tú → you drink
> ólaim or ólann mé → I drink
> ólann Séamus → James drinks
>
> bris → break
> briseann tú → you break
> brisim or briseann mé → I break
> briseann Máire → Mary breaks

Verbs with more than one syllable fall under the "second conjugation" of Irish verbs. In this case, endings are not always simply added on to the end of root verbs;

rather, the root verbs may have to be changed.

For those root verbs that end in –aigh and –igh, the last syllable must be removed before the present tense stems can be added. For root verbs that end in –ail or –il, –ain or –in, –air or –ir, and –ais or –is, these endings are removed **except for the last letter**. For example, the verb oscail becomes oscl– before present tense roots are added. The table below shows the endings added to these verbs.

Pronoun	Broad Ending	Slender Ending
mé	-aíonn mé or -aím	-íonn mé or -ím
tú	-aíonn tú	-íonn tú
sé	-aíonn sé	-íonn sé
sí	-aíonn sí	-íonn sí
muid	-aíonn muid or -aímid	-íonn muid or -ímid
sibh	-aíonn sibh	-íonn sibh
siad	-aíonn siad	-íonn siad

Once the root word has been transformed using the methods described above, these endings can be added.

oibrigh → work
oibríonn tú → you work
oibrím or oibríonn mé → I work

Not including *bí*, there are ten irregular verbs in Irish. Only six are covered in this chapter, but as more are introduced throughout this workbook, they will be noted.

abair → deireann
déan → déanann
faigh → faigheann
feic → feiceann
ithe → itheann
téigh → téann

Present Tense Review

→ When describing a noun, the verb *tá*, is used, meaning is. When combined with the pronouns *mé* and *muid*, contractions can be formed.
→ The present tense is formed by adding endings onto the root forms of verbs. These endings are determined by the amount of syllables the verb has and whether it is broad or slender.
→ Sometimes, changes must be made to the root forms of verbs in the second conjugation.
→ Not including *tá*, ten irregular Irish verbs exist, six of which were covered in this lesson.

Conjugate each of these verbs in the present tense based on the pronoun in parenthesis.

1) déan (you)
2) oibrigh (you *pl.*)
3) faigh (we)
4) téigh (they)
5) úsáid (I)
6) feic (she)

Translate each of these sentences into Irish.

7) The people are red.
8) John is tall.
9) He says words.
10) We drink milk.
11) We are tall.
12) You use money.
13) You *(pl.)* go.
14) I see the family.

· 5 ·
Adjectives and Questions

Vocabulary

IRISH SINGULAR		ENGLISH
an	/on/	very
bán	/bawn/	white
bándearg	/bawn-dare-ugg/	pink
beag	/bee-ugg/	small
buí	/bwee/	yellow
ceart	/kairt/	right
droch	/drock/	bad
dubh	/dove/	black
gearr	/gair/	short
glas	/gloss/	green
gorm	/gore-um/	blue
óg	/ohg/	young
maith	/ma/	good
mícheart	/mic-hyairt/	wrong
mór	/more/	big
nua	/new-uh/	new
oráiste	/or-osh-tay/	orange
ró	/row/	very
sásta	/sawsta/	satisfied
sean	/shawn/	old

Using adjectives

Unlike English, in Irish, adjectives come after the noun. In English, we would say the small house, but in Irish, this phrase would become *an teach beag*, which literally translates to *the house small*.

In addition, Irish adjectives are lenited after feminine nouns.

> an fear mór → the big man
> an mhuintir mhór → the big family

Because *muintir*, meaning family, is a feminine word, the adjective *mór* was lenited. Adjectives also take on plural forms when they follow plural nouns. An *-a* is added onto the end of adjectives that end in a broad consonant, while *-e* is added onto adjectives ending in a slender consonant. Adjectives that end in vowels do not undergo any changes.

> an cailín gearr → the short girl
> na cailíní gearra → the short girls
>
> an scoil buí → the yellow school
> na scoileanna buí → the yellow schools

Special cases

Certain adjectives do not follow the rules described above. One such case involves the words *droch* and *sean*. These adjectives do not come after the noun to which they relate; rather, they come before the noun and form a compound word. In this case, the noun is also lenited.

> fear óg → young man
> seanfhear → old man

The adjectives *an* and *ró* are also placed before the noun. A hyphen is put between *an* and the preceding noun in all cases, and a hyphen is put between *ró* and the noun when the noun begins with a vowel. Once again, both of these adjectives lenite the noun to which they belong.

 an-mhor → very big
 rómhor → too big

 an-óg → very young
 ró-óg → too young

Finally, the word *maith* is typically not used alone when describing a noun. In most cases, *go* is added before *maith* to form the word well.

 go maith → well
 Táim go maith → I am well

Questions

Asking questions in Irish is pretty simple. Here's an example:

 Séamus: *An bhfeiceann tú an bainne?* (Do you see the milk?)
 Máire: *Feicim.* (I see)

To form a question in the present tense, *An* must be added before the verb, which then adds eclipsis. In Séamus's case, he took the present tense verb *feiceann*, put *An* before the verb, and added eclipsis.

Responding to questions get a little bit trickier. In Irish, there are no words for **yes** or **no**. Instead, when asked a question, the corresponding affirmative or negative verb is used.

 Séamus: *An itheann tú arán?*
 Máire: *Ithim.*

When asked if she eats bread, instead of saying "yes," Máire responded by saying "I eat." Now, if Máire wanted to respond to the question negatively and say that she does not eat bread, she would say "I do not eat." This is formed by adding *ní*, meaning not, before the verb.

Séamus: *An itheann tú arán?*
Máire: *Ní ithim.*

The only verb to which these rules do not pertain is *tá* (is). When used in questions, *tá* takes on its interrogative form, which is *bhfuil*.

an bhfuil...? → is...?

Questions starting with *an bhfuil* can either be answered with *tá*, literally meaning "is" in this case, or *níl*, which literally means "not."

Bríd: *An bhfuil an bainne bán?* (Is the milk white?)
Seán: *Tá.* (Yes.)
Máire: *Níl.* (No.)

When the subject of the sentence is a pronoun, this pronoun is included in the answer. Like with *tá*, the pronouns *mé* and *muid* form contractions when combined with *níl*, becoming *nílim* and *nílimid*, respectively.

Séamus: *An bhfuil tú go maith?*
Máire: *Táim* or *tá mé*
Bríd: *Nílim* or *níl mé*

Adjectives and Questions Review

→ Irish adjectives come after the noun, except in the cases of *sean*, *droch*, *an-*, and *ró*. These adjectives come before the noun, and in most cases combine with it to form a compound word.
→ Adjectives are lenited following feminine nouns. They also must be pluralized when following plural nouns.
→ Irish questions are formed by adding *An* before a present tense verb. Eclipsis must also be added to the verb.
→ There are no words for "yes" or "no" in Irish. Instead, the corresponding affirmative or negative verb is used.
→ The interrogative form of the verb *tá* is *bhfuil*. Questions with *bhfuil* can be answered with either *tá* or *níl*.

Translate each of the phrases below.

1) the big houses
2) the small restaurant
3) the old women
4) the green money
5) too small
6) very new
7) the orange milk
8) the wrong word

Fill in the missing questions and answers. Be creative!

Séamus: An ólann tú an bainne?
Máire: _____.

Bríd: _____?
Seán: Feicim.

Séamus: An bhfuil tú ceart?
Máire: _____.

Bríd: _____?
Seán: Nílim.

· 6 ·
PREPOSITIONS

Vocabulary

IRISH SINGULAR		ENGLISH
ag	/ag/	at
ar	/ar/	on
as	/ass/	out of
chuig	/kwig/	to
de	/day/	off
do	/doe/	for
faoi	/fwee/	about
i	/ih/	in
idir	/idjer/	between
le	/lay/	with
ó	/oh/	from
roimh	/riv/	before
thar	/har/	over
trí	/tree/	through

Basic prepositions

In English, prepositions are used to describe relationships between things. Irish prepositions also have this function, among others. The table above outlines the fourteen most common Irish prepositions.

> le → with
> Tá tú le Séamus → You are with James

This is the most basic use of the Irish preposition, as well as the most common. The next few sections outline the most complex uses of these terms.

Prepositional pronouns

In Irish, when prepositions are used with pronouns, the two words form a contraction called a prepositional pronoun. For example, instead of saying *le mé* to express **with me** in Irish, the contraction *liom* is used.

> Tá sé liom → He is with me

The table below shows the contractions that are created when each preposition is combined with each pronoun.

	mé	tú	sé	sí	muid	sibh	siad
ag	agam	agat	aige	aici	againn	agaibh	acu
ar	orm	ort	air	uirthi	orainn	oraibh	orthu
as	asam	asat	as	aisti	asainn	asaibh	astu
chuig	chugam	chugat	chuige	chuici	chugainn	chugaibh	chucu
de	díom	díot	de	di	dínn	díbh	díobh
do	dom	duit	dó	di	dúinn	daoibh	dóibh
faoi	fúm	fút	faoi	fúithi	fúinn	fúibh	fúthu
i	ionam	ionat	ann	inti	ionainn	ionaibh	iontu
idir	-	-	-	-	eadrainn	eadraibh	eatarthu
le	liom	leat	leis	léi	linn	libh	leo
ó	uaim	uait	uaidh	uaithi	uainn	uaibh	uathu
roimh	romham	romhat	roimhe	roimpi	romhainn	romhaibh	rompu
thar	tharam	tharat	thairis	thairsti	tharainn	tharaibh	tharstu
trí	tríom	tríot	tríd	tríthi	trínn	tríbh	tríothu

These prepositional pronouns may look very daunting at first, but as you become more familiar with their use, they will become much easier to remember.

The preposition *ag*

The most commonly used preposition in the Irish language is *ag*, meaning at. Typically, *ag* is used when describing the location of a noun.

> Tá mé ag an scoil → I am at the school
> Oibríonn tú ag an bhialann → You work at the restaurant

This preposition is also essential in expressing ownership. There is no verb for "to have" in Irish; thus, *ag* is used instead. For example, the sentence "The boy has milk" would be translated to *Tá bainne ag an buachaill*, literally meaning "Milk is at the boy."

> Tá airgead ag an bhean → The woman has money *(money is at the woman)*
> Tá cairde ag an fear → The man has friends *(friends are at the man)*
> An bhfuil arán ag Seán? → Does John have bread? *(is there bread at John?)*

Prepositional pronouns are also used in this form, as can be seen below:

> Tá bainne agam → I have milk *(milk is at me)*
> Tá an teach aige → He has the house *(the house is at him)*
> An bhfuil airgead acu? → Do they have money? *(is there money at them?)*

The preposition *ar*

Another common Irish pronoun is *ar*, meaning on. Like *ag*, this can be used in a literal way and an abstract way.

> Tá an fear ar an teach → The man is on the house
> Tá tú orm → You are on me

Ar can also convey obligation when used with the root form of a verb. In Irish, the sentence "You must go" is translated to *Tá ort téigh*, which is literally "It is on you to go."

> Tá ar Séamus abair → James must speak *(it is on James to speak)*

Tá orm oibrigh → I must work *(it is on me to work)*

The preposition *le*

Le, meaning with, also has an abstract usage. When used with the adjective *maith*, *le* can express a sense of like or dislike.

Is maith liom → I like *(is good with me)*
Ní maith liom → I do not like *(is not good with me)*

These phrases use a verb form called the *copula*, which will be described in a later lesson. For now, just remember the general phrases *Is maith le* and *Ní maith le*.

Is maith leat bainne → You like milk *(milk is good with you)*
Is maith le Bríd arán → Bridget likes bread

Ní maith leis uisce → He does not like water *(water is not good with him)*
Ní maith le Séamus daoine → James does not like people

An maith leat airgead? → Do you like money? *(is money good with you?)*
An maith le Máire mé? → Does Mary like me?

The preposition ó

Finally, we'll take a look at the preposition *ó*, meaning from. Like each of the previous prepositions, *ó* can be used in two ways. Here's an example of its literal use:

Oibríonn sé ó theach → He works from a house

Ó can also express wants. In Irish, the English sentence "I want bread" is translated to *Tá arán orm*, literally meaning "Bread is from me."

Tá bainne uainn → We want milk *(milk is from us)*
Tá airgead ó Seán → John wants money *(money is from John)*

Though there are certainly many more uses of prepositions, the four described above are most commonly used in conversational Irish.

Prepositions Review

→ When prepositions are used with pronouns, they form prepositional pronouns.
→ The preposition *ag*, meaning at, can be used to express ownership.
→ The preposition *ar*, meaning on, can be used to express obligation.
→ The preposition *le*, meaning with, can be used to express likes and dislikes through the phrase *Is maith le*.
→ The preposition *ó*, meaning from, can be used to express want.

Translate each of the sentences below.

1) You have a house.
2) He must eat.
3) Do they like Irish?
4) I want bread and you want water.

5) An bhfuil bialann agat?
6) Tá uirthi feic.
7) Ní maith leí na buachaillí.
8) An bhfuil cairde ort?

Find and fix the errors in the conversation below. Be careful - some sentences contain multiple errors.

Séamus: An bhfuil úll ag tú?
Bríd: Níl maith le mé úlla glas.
Séamus: Tá maith le tú úlla dearga?
Bríd: Is maith le mé. Tá ar mé ithe.

·7·
The Present Participle

Vocabulary

IRISH SINGULAR		IRISH PLURAL		ENGLISH
mo	/mow/			my
do	/doe/	bhur	/vur/	your
a	/ah/			his/her/their
ár	/ar/			our
léigh	/lay/			read
rith	/rih/			run
scríobh	/skreev/			write
siúl	/shool/			walk
snámh	/snav/			swim
tabhair	/tower/			give
tar	/tar/			come
bord	/board/	boird	/byord/	table
carr	/car/	carranna	/car-ana/	car
doras	/doris/	doirse	/door-shay/	door
fuinneog	/fwin-og/	fuinneoga	/fwin-oga/	window
leabhar	/laow-er/	leabhair	/laow-ra/	book
teilifís	/tell-ih-feesh/	teilifíseáin	/tell-ih-feesh-shawn/	television

Possessive adjectives

Though complex Irish possessives are expressed using the genitive case, possessive adjectives are used to express words like "my" and "our." A list of these adjectives is provided in the table at the beginning of the chapter.

The adjectives *mo* and *do* cause the word that they are describing to be lenited, while *ár* and *bhur* add eclipsis to the following word. Depending on its direct translation, *a* can cause either one of these.

> when *a* means his → lenition
> when *a* means her → no change
> when *a* means their → eclipsis

Because these changes depend on the use of *a*, the words "his," "her," and "their" can be differentiated by looking at the words they are describing.

> mo bhord → my table
> do charr → your car
> a dhoras → his door
> a duine → her people
> ár dteilifís → our television
> bhur bhfuinneog → your *(pl)* window
> a mbainne → their milk

More irregulars

Two more irregulars, *tabhair* and *tar*, were introduced in this chapter's vocabulary table. Their present tense conjugations are listed below:

> tabhair → tugann
> tar → tagann

The present participle

In English, the present participle is used to create a continuous tense through a verb form ending in "-ing." In Irish, the present participle is used in the same way; however, forming this tense is much easier.

Instead of adding a certain ending to the end of Irish verbs, the verb *ag* is used in conjunction with the verb *tá* to form the present participle.

> Tá Séamus ag rith → James is running
> Tá siad ag scríobh an leabhar → They are writing the book
> Táim ag abair le mo chairde → I am talking with my friends

As usual, the verb *tá* is placed at the beginning of the sentence, followed by the subject. The present participle form of a verb is then created using *ag*, and this is placed after the subject.

Present Participle Review

- → Possessive adjectives are used in conjunction with nouns to express ownership.
- → The present participle is used to create an "-ing" ending with the verb *ag*.
- → The participle must always be expressed with the verb *bí*.

Translate each of the phrases below.

1) do fhuinneog
2) a fuinneog
3) a dhoras
4) mo dhoras
5) a gcairde
6) bhur gcairde

Translate the following sentences into English.

7) Tá tú ag úsáid do theilifís.
8) Ní maith liom na fuinneoga san teach.
9) Tá mo bainne agaibh.
10) Tagann siad chugam leis an bhean nua.
11) Tá bhur boird móra uaim.
12) Oibríonn sí san bhialann le Bríd.
13) Feiceann muid an Sasana as ár dteach.
14) Táimid ag snámh.

*Note: when *sa* is used in conjunction with *an*, the word *san* is formed.
*Note: when *le* is used in conjunction with *an*, the word *leis* is used.

·8·
the copula

Vocabulary

IRISH SINGULAR		IRISH PLURAL		ENGLISH
ach	/akk/			but
agus	/augus/			and
go	/go/			to
nó	/no/			or
athair	/ah-her/	aithreacha	/ah-hreeka/	father
dalta	/dollta/	daltaí	/dolltee/	student
dochtúir	/dock-tur/	dochtúirí	/dock-turee/	doctor
Éireannach	/air-ih-knock/	Éireannaigh	/air-in-aigh/	Irishman
feirmeoir	/far-mower/	feirmeoirí	/far-mower-ee/	farmer
garda	/gar-duh/	gardaí	/gar-dee/	policeman
iníon (f)	/in-ian/	iníonacha	/in-ian-acka/	daughter
innealtóir	/in-ail-tor/	innealtóirí	/in-ail-toree/	engineer
mac	/mack/	mic	/mic/	son
máthair (f)	/mah-her/	mathareacha	/mah-hericka/	mother
Meiriceánach	/mary-con-ock/	Meiriceánaigh	/mary-con-aigh/	American
múinteoir	/moon-chore/	múinteoirí	/moon-chor-ee/	teacher
rúnaí	/rew-knee/	rúnaithe	/rew-nih-hay/	secretary
Sasanach	/sass-a-knock/	Sasanaigh	/sass-an-aigh/	Englishman
Taoiseach	/tee-shock/	Taoisigh	/tee-sheeg/	Irish prime minister

Using the *copula*

As was mentioned in the lesson on the present tense, the copula is the second form of "to be" in Irish. This tense is used when both the object and subject of a sentence are nouns or pronouns. For example, the sentence "She is an engineer" would require the use of the copula, as "she" is being compared to an engineer.

In terms of grammar, the copula does not follow the traditional Irish VSO sentence structure. Instead, it follows a VOS order, in which the verb is followed by the object *and then* the subject.

> Is innealtóir í → She is an engineer

When using the copula, the verb *is* is used in the place of *tá*. Following that is the object of the sentence, which is "engineer" in this case. After this comes a pronoun; *sé, sí,* and *siad* become *é, í,* and *iad*.

> Is buachaill mé → I am a boy
> Is Meiriceánach tú → You are an American
> Is daltaí iad → They are students

The *copula* with the definite article

When used with the definite article (*an* and *na*), the format of the copula becomes a little bit different.

> Is í an dochtúir í → She is <u>the</u> doctor

The definite article is **never** allowed to be in between *is* and the pronoun; thus, it must be placed after both of these. Notice how a second *í* is added to the end of the sentence above. This must be done with the pronouns *é, í,* and *iad*.

Another format of the copula is used with the pronouns *mé, tú,* and *muid*. In this case, the emphatic forms of these pronouns are used. *Mé, tú,* and *muid* become *mise, tusa,* and *muide*.

> Is mise an dochtúir → I am the doctor
> Is tusa an Taoiseach → You are the Irish prime minister

The *copula* without pronouns

The *copula* can also be used without pronouns when comparing two nouns.

    Is múinteoir é an fear → The man is a teacher

This is exactly the same as the basic form of the *copula*, except the subject of the sentence is placed after a proleptic pronoun. Think of the pronoun in this case as a placeholder, as the *é* in the sentence above is simply "holding the place" of *an fear*.

    Is dochtúir í an cailín → The girl is a doctor
    Is Sasanaigh iad na daoine → The people are Englishmen

As was mentioned above, the definite article is never allowed to be in between *is* and the pronoun. Thus, if the object of the sentence contains a definite article, it must be placed after the proleptic (placeholder) pronoun.

    Is é Séamus an rúnaí → James is the secretary

Notice how in this form, the object of the sentence, *rúnaí*, follows the subject of the sentence, *Séamus*. This occurs because the subject of the sentence must always directly follow the proleptic pronoun.

Like many Irish grammatical concepts, the *copula* seems to be extremely confusing at first. Because there is no *copula* in the English language, it can initially be very tricky to understand; however, as you use this concept more and more, it will become much easier to remember the rules surrounding its usage.

The negative *copula*

The negative *copula* is extremely simple. Instead of the verb *is*, the verb *ní* is used in this tense to express the negative.

    Ní dochtúir mé → I am not a doctor

Copula Review

→ The *copula* is used when comparing two nouns or pronouns, and the verb *is* is used in the place of *tá*.
→ The basic *copula* follows a VOS word order. In this form, *sé*, *sí*, and *siad* become *é*, *í*, and *iad*.
→ The definite article is never allowed to be in between *is* and the pronoun, so it is placed directly after the pronoun. The emphatic forms of *mé*, *tú*, and *muid* are used in this scenario.
→ Without pronouns, the subject of the sentence is placed directly after a "placeholder" pronoun in the *copula*. The subject of the sentence must always follow this placeholder.

Determine whether each of the sentences requires tá *or the* copula. *Then, translate them into English.*

1) The men are tall.
2) He is a teacher.
3) They are not men.
4) The men are too short.
5) Apples are red.
6) I am the engineer.

Use the copula to translate these sentences.

7) You are an Irishman.
8) He is the teacher.
9) I am the student.
10) The person is a secretary.
11) The boy is a son.
12) The man is not a grandfather.
13) John is the engineer.
14) Bridget is the policewoman.

·9·
the past tense

Vocabulary

IRISH SINGULAR		IRISH PLURAL		ENGLISH
bád	/bod/	báid	/badj/	boat
bia	/bee-ah/	bianna	/bee-ana/	food
bóthar	/bah-her/	bóithre	/bah-hree/	road
capall	/cah-pull/	capaill	/cah-pill/	horse
cat	/caht/	cait	/cathj/	cat
feoil *(l)*	/fee-ull/	feolta	/fee-ulta/	meat
glasra	/glass-ruh/	glasraí	/glass-ree/	vegetable
madra	/mah-druh/	madraí	/mah-dree/	dog
rothar	/rah-her/	rothair	/rah-hair/	bicycle
seomra	/showm-ruh/	seomraí	/showm-ree/	room
toradh	/tore-uh/	torthaí	/tore-hee/	fruit
beir	/bear/			catch
clois	/cloy-sh/			hear
dún	/done/			close
imirt	/imert/			play
oscail	/os-cul/			open
tiomáint	/tih-moint/			drive

To be

Just like in the present tense, the Irish past tense also has two forms of "to be." The past tense form of *tá* is *bhí*, pronounced /vee/. The past tense form of the copula, *is*, is *ba*.

Bhí mé gearr → I was short
Ba dochtúir í → She was a doctor

When *bhí* is used with *muid*, the contraction *bhíomar* is formed.

Bhíomar óg → We were young

In the past tense, the negative form of *bhí* is *ní raibh*, and the negative form of *ba* is *níor*.

Ní raibh mé go maith → I was not well
Níor múinteoir iad → They were not teachers

The past tense

Forming the past tense is much simpler than forming the present tense in that instead of adding an ending to the root forms of verbs, the root forms are simply transformed in the past tense. Though there are first and second conjugations of Irish past tense verbs, the verbs in both of these categories undergo near-identical changes.

When forming the past tense with verbs that begin with consonants, the root form of the verb is simply lenited. Verbs that begin with vowels are not lenited; rather, they are prefixed with *d'*. Verbs that start with *f* are both lenited and prefixed with *d'*.

dhún mé → I closed
thiomáint siad → they drove
d'oscail tú → you closed
d'ól sí → she drank

Irregular verbs

The last two irregular verbs, *beir* and *clois*, were introduced in the table above. Below are their present tense conjugations:

beir → beireann
clois → cloiseann

The past tense forms of all ten irregular verbs are shown below.

abair → dúirt	beir → rug
clois → chuala	déan → rinne
faigh → fuair	feic → chonaic
ith → d'ith	tabhair → thug
tar → tháinig	téigh → chauigh

While a few of these conjugations look extremely similar to their root verbs, most of these bear no resemblance to their root forms. Thus, the past tense conjugations of these ten irregular verbs must be memorized.

The negative past tense

Past tense verbs can be made negative by adding *níor* before the past tense verb. Of course, the past tense verb is still lenited when in this form.

Níor thiománt sé → He did not drive
Níor d'imirt an madra → The dog did not play

There are a few exceptions to this rule in which the word *níor* is not used:

abair → ní dúirt	déan → ní dhearna
faigh → ní bhfuair	feic → ní fhaca
téigh → ní dheachaigh	*bí → ní raibh*

Questions

While in the present tense form, questions are asked using the word *an*, in the Irish past tense, the word *ar* is used instead.

Ar dhún tú an doras? → Did you close the door?

Ar d'oscail Bríd na doirse? → Did Bridget close the doors?

Once again, the five verbs that did not use *níor* in the negative form do not use *ar* when asking questions in the past tense.

abair → an ndúirt...?	déan → an ndearna...?
faigh → an bhfuair...?	feic → an bhfaca...?
téigh → an ndeachaigh...?	bí → an raibh...?

Past Tense Review

→ In the past tense, the present tense verb *tá* becomes *bhí*, while the verb *is* becomes *ba*. The negative forms of these verbs are *ní raibh* and *níor*, respectively.

→ The Irish past tense is formed by leniting the root form of the original verb. Verbs that begin with vowels are simply prefixed with *D'*, and verbs that begin with *f* are lenited and prefixed with *D'*.

→ The ten irregular Irish verbs have drastically different past tense forms, each of which should be memorized.

→ The negative past tense is formed by adding *níor* before the past tense verb. Six exceptions exist to this rule.

→ Past tense questions are formed by using the word *ar* instead of *an*. The same six verb exceptions exist for this grammatical concept.

Turn each present tense sentence into past tense.

1) Itheann mé arán agus feoil.
2) Tá tú ag tiomáint do rothar ar an bóthar.
3) Ní ólann muid bainne.
4) Scríobhann Séamus leabhar san teach.
5) An bhfeiceann tú mo chapall?
6) Cloisím na cait.
7) Deireann Bríd le Séamus agus Máire.
8) Oibríonn an múinteoir san scoil.

Translate the paragraph below.

Ba múinteoir é Séamus agus d'oibrigh sé san scoil. Níor mhaith le Séamus buachaillí nó cailíní, ach bhí sé go maith le daoine óg. Léigh sé leabhair le na daltaí.

Using your knowledge of the past tense, translate the conversation below to English.

    Máire: An ndúirt tú le Seán faoi a mhadra?
    Bríd: Ní dúirt mé.
    Máire: Tá ort abair leis. Ni maith liom a mhadra.

Translate the conversation below into Irish.

    James: You went to the restaurant with Bridget. Did you eat meat?
    John: I did not, but I drank milk and water.
    James: Was Bridget satisfied with her food?
    John: She was; she liked her food.
    James: Did she eat meat or vegetables?
    John: She did not eat vegetables or meat – she ate bread.

·10·
the imperative

Vocabulary

IRISH SINGULAR		IRISH PLURAL		ENGLISH
abhaile	/a-vah-lay/			home
am	/owm/	amanna	/owmana/	time
clé *(l)*	/clay/			left
deis *(l)*	/daysh/			right
éadach	/ee-a-dock/	éadaí	/ee-a-dee/	clothing
rud	/rud/	rudaí	/rudee/	thing
ciúin	/cue-in/			quiet
roinnt	/roint/			some
seo	/show/			this
sín	/shin/			that
cas	/cass/			turn
ceannaigh	/can-ig/			buy
lig	/lig/			let
stad	/stad/			stop
suigh	/see-ig/			sit

Using commands

The imperative form of a verb is simply the command form. For example, in the phrase "Buy some meat for me!" the verb "buy" would be in its imperative form, as it is being used as a command.

Forming the imperative in Irish is extremely easy. The *second person singular* form is used when the command is directed at one person. To form this, simply take the root form of the verb - that's it!

>Téigh abhaile → Go home
>Bí ciúin → Be quiet
>Ceannaigh roinnt feoil dom → Buy some meat for me

Forming the *second person plural* is a little bit harder. This is used when the command is being directed at multiple people. To form this in the first conjugation (one-syllable verbs), *-aigí* is added to verbs with broad endings and *-igí* is added to verbs with slender endings.

>Rithigí ar an mbóthar → Run on the road
>Ólaigí bhur mbia → Eat your food

In the second conjugation (multi-syllable verbs), if the verb ends in *-aigh* or *-igh*, this part of the verb is removed to create a modified root form. If the verb ends in *-ail/-il*, *-ais/-is*, *-air/-ir*, or *-ais/-is*, these parts of verb are removed **except** for the last letter to create the modified root form. The endings *-aigí* or *-igí* are then added to the modified root form.

>Ceannaigí an bainne → Buy the milk
>Osclaigí an doras → Open the door

Negative commands

To form negative commands, the word *ná*, meaning "do not," is simply added in front of the affirmative command.

>Ná súil leis → Don't walk with him
>Ná dúnaigí an fhuinneog → Don't close the window

Irregular commands

While all of the Irish irregular verbs follow the rules of *second person singular commands*, irregular forms of these verbs are used when forming *second person plural commands*.

>Abair liom → Talk with me
>Bí sásta → Be satisfied

The irregular imperative verbs are listed below. You may notice that the verb *clois* is missing from this list – this is because commands cannot be formed with this verb, as it means "to hear."

abair → abraigí	beir → beirigí
bí → bígí	déan → déeanaigí
faigh → faighigí	feic → feicigí
ith → ithigí	tabhair → tugaigí
tar → tagaigí	téigh → téigí

Imperative Review

- → Commands are formed using the imperative form of verbs.
- → The *second person singular* is directed at one person, and is formed by using the root form of the verb.
- → The *second person plural* is formed in the first conjugation by adding *-aigí* or *-igí* to the root form of the verb.
- → The *second person plural* is formed in the second conjugation by removing certain endings to create a modified root form. The endings *-aigí* or *-igí* are then added to this modified root form.
- → Negative commands are formed by adding *ná*, meaning not.
- → Ten irregular commands in the *second person plural* form exist in Irish.

Translate the sentences below in both the second person singular *and* second person plural *forms.*

1) Eat your food!
2) Drink the milk!

3) Walk the dog!
4) Buy some clothes for him!
5) Don't talk with the policeman!
6) Don't come home with James!
7) Swim with the horse!
8) Give some fruit to the teacher!

Translate the following conversation.

Seán: Ar gceannaigh tú bainne?
Bríd: Níor cheannaigh mé bainne, ach tá uisce agam.
Seán: Níl uisce uaim! Ceannaigh bainne dom!

· 11 ·
the future tense

Vocabulary

IRISH SINGULAR		IRISH PLURAL		ENGLISH
aerfort	/air-fort/	aerfoirt	/air-foirt/	airport
biachlár	/bee-ah-clar/	biachláir	/bee-ah-clair/	menu
bricfeasta	/brick-fasta/			breakfast
bríste	/bree-stay/	brístí	/bree-stee/	pants
bróg *(l)*	/brohg/	bróga	/brohga/	shoe
dinnéar	/din-ayir/			dinner
fuisce	/fwiscay/	fuiscí	/fwish-key/	whiskey
léine *(l)*	/lay-nay/	léinte	/lain-tee/	shirt
lón	/lown/			lunch
margadh	/mar-guh/	margaí	/mar-gee/	market
nuachtán	/new-ock-ton/	nuachtáin	/new-ock-tin/	newspaper
óstán	/aw-ston/	óstáin	/awsh-ton/	hotel
páiste	/posh-tah/	páistí	/posh-tee/	child
tae	/tay/			tea
ubh *(l)*	/of/	uibheacha	/ubb-ik-ah/	egg
athraigh	/at-rye/			change
díol	/dee-ull/			sell
foghlaim	/fogh-liam/			learn
íoc	/ee-ok/			pay
troid	/teroid/			fight

To be

As we've seen with the past and present tenses, there are two forms of "to be" – the future tense is no different. *Tá* in the future tense is *beidh*, pronounced /bee/. The copula stays the same as the present tense in the future tense. The negative form of *beidh* is simply *ní bheidh*, while once again, the negative copula is identical in the present and future tenses.

    Beidh mé ard → I will be tall
    Beidh siad óg → They will be young

The future tense

Like the present tense, the future tense is formed by adding an ending to the root verb. The endings for first conjugation verbs (one syllable) are shown in the table below.

Pronoun	Broad Ending	Slender Ending
mé	-faidh mé	-fidh mé
tú	-faidh tú	-fidh tú
sé	-faidh sé	-fidh sé
sí	-faidh sí	-fidh sí
muid	-faidh muid or -faimid	-fidh muid or -fimid
sibh	-faidh sibh	-fidh sibh
siad	-faidh siad	-fidh siad

As usual, depending on whether the last vowel in the verb is broad or slender, the endings above are added onto one syllable verbs when forming the future tense.

    Ólfaidh mé bainne → I will drink milk
    Brisfidh tú an fhuinneog → You will break the window
    Íocfaimid do bhricfeasta → We will buy your breakfast

The endings differ for second conjugation (multi-syllable) verbs. The endings in the table below are added onto verbs in this class. For those root verbs that end in -aigh and -igh, the -aigh and -igh must be removed before the future tense stems can be added. For root verbs that end in -ail or -il, -ain or -in, -air or -ir, and -ais or -is, these endings are removed **except** for the last letter before an ending can be added.

Pronoun	Broad Ending	Slender Ending
mé	-óidh mé	-eoidh mé
tú	-óidh tú	-eoidh tú
sé	-óidh sé	-eoidh sé
sí	-óidh sí	-eoidh sí
muid	-óidh muid or -óimid	-eoidh muid or -eoimid
sibh	-óidh sibh	-eoidh sibh
siad	-óidh siad	-eoidh siad

Once again, once the root word has been transformed using the methods described above, these endings can be added.

Athróidh sí a leine → She will change her shirt
Osclóidh sibh na doirse → They will close the doors
Ceannóidh mé an bainne → I will buy the milk

Irregular verbs

The future tense forms of the ten irregular verbs are shown below.

abair → déarfaidh
clois → cloisfidh
faigh → gheobhaidh
ith → íosfaidh
tar → tiocfaidh

beir → béarfaidh
déan → déanfaidh
feic → feicfidh
tabhair → tabharfaidh
téigh → rachaidh

The negative future tense

Future tense verbs are negated by adding *ní* before the verb. This lenites the future tense form of the verb.

Ní throidfidh sé → He will not fight
Ní rithfidh siad → They will not run

Questions

Like in the present tense, future tense question are asked using the word *an*. This causes the future tense verb to become eclipsed.

> An ndúnfidh tú an fhuinneog? → Will you close the window?
> An ndíolfaidh Séamus a mhadra? → Will James sell his dog?

Future Tense Review

- → In the future tense, the present tense verb *tá* becomes *beidh*, with its negative being *ní bheidh*. The present and future tense copula are identical.
- → The Irish future tense is formed by adding certain endings onto the root forms of verbs depending on their conjugation and whether they are broad or slender.
- → The ten irregular Irish verbs have different future tense forms.
- → The negative future tense is formed by adding *ní* before the future tense verb.
- → Future tense questions are formed by using the word *an*.

Translate the sentences below.

1) I will eat my food.
2) You will buy meat for me.
3) They will not run on the road.
4) Will she drive her car?
5) We will pay for it.
6) Will you come with me?
7) Will she fight with him?
8) You *(pl)* will be quiet.

·12·
Common Phrases

Vocabulary

IRISH SINGULAR		ENGLISH
brón	/br-oan/	sadness
Dia	/djia/	God
Muire	/mur-uh/	the Virgin Mary
toil	/toll/	desire
cé	/kay/	who
conas	/conus/	how
fáilte	/fall-chay/	welcome
sláinte	/slawn-cha/	health
slán	/slawn/	goodbye

Hello and goodbye

In Irish, there is no specific word for hello. Instead, the greeting *Dia duit* is used.

    Dia duit → God be with you

Literally, this means "God be with you" – however, it carries the same significance as the English word "hello." To respond to this, the phrase *Dia's Muire duit* is used.

Dia's Muire duit → God and Mary be with you

This is simply the proper response to *Dia duit*, and is pronounced /djia smur-uh djwit/.

Séamus: Dia duit!
Máire: Dia's Muire duit!

To say goodbye, the Irish word *slán* is used.

How are you?

In Irish, there are two ways to ask how somebody is. These ways vary based on region. In most of Ireland, the phrase *Conas atá tú?* is used.

Conas atá tú? → How are you?

However, in the Connaught region of Ireland, the phrase *Cén chaoi bhfuil tú?*, pronounced /kay chay vwil too/, is used. This phrase may also be heard elsewhere in Ireland.

Cén chaoi bhfuil tú? → How are you?

Common replies to these questions are listed below:

Tá mé go maith → I am well
Tá mé sásta → I am satisfied (similar to *I am happy*)
Tá mé go dona → I am bad

Other common phrases

A few more Irish phrases, along with their pronunciations, are listed below.

Go raibh maith agat → Thank you   /go rah mah agut/
Tá fáilte romhat → You're welcome   /taw fall-chay wrote/

Le do thoil → Please /lay dow hull/
Tá brón orm → I am sorry /taw ber-owm agum/
Sláinte! → Cheers! /slawn-cha/

Conclusion

Though there are many more grammatical concepts and much more vocabulary in the Irish language, this workbook has provided you with a thorough overview of *an Ghaeilge*. The Irish language is considered to be one of the hardest in the world to learn, yet with it comes a renewed sense of understanding for the Irish people and Irish culture. I wish you all the best as you continue your journey through the Irish language. *Slán!*

answer key

Lesson One

1) fhorc; bhforc
2) shpúnóg; spúnóg
3) shcian; scian
4) phláta; bpláta
5) chupán; gcupán
6) naipcín; naipcín
7) broad
8) broad
9) slender
10) broad
11) broad
12) slender

Lesson Two

1) an fear; the man
2) an t-uisce; the water
3) na bhialanna; the restaurants
4) an teach; the house
5) na daoine; the people
6) an Ghaeilge; the Irish language
7) na cailíní; the girls
8) na mná; the women

Lesson Three

1) mé
2) í
3) sé
4) muid
5) sibh
6) iad
7) sí
8) tú féin

Lesson Four

1) déanann tú
2) oibríonn sibh
3) faigheann muid or faighimid
4) téann siad
5) úsáideann mé or úsáidim
6) feiceann sí
7) Tá na daoine dearga.
8) Tá Seán ard.
9) Deireann sé focail.
10) Ólaimid bainne.
11) Táimid ard.
12) Úsáideann tú airgead.
13) Téann sibh.
14) Feicim an mhuintir.

Lesson Five

1) na tithe móra
2) an bhialann bheag
3) na seanmná
4) an airgead glas
5) róbheag
6) an-nua
7) an bainne oráiste
8) an focal mícheart

ANSWERS MAY VARY FOR PART II

Lesson Six

1) Tá teach agat.
2) Tá air ithe.
3) An mhaith leo an Ghaeilge?
4) Tá arán uaim agus tá uisce uait.
5) Do you have a restaurant?
6) She must see.
7) She doesn't like the boys.
8) Do you have friends?

Séamus: An bhfuil úll agat?
Bríd: Ní maith liom úlla glasa.
Séamus: An maith leat úlla dearga?
Bríd: Is maith liom. Tá orm ithe.

Lesson Seven

1) your window
2) her window
3) his door
4) my door
5) their friends
6) your friends
7) You are using your television.
8) I don't like the windows in the house.
9) You have my milk.
10) They come to me with the new woman.
11) I want your big tables.
12) She works in the restaurant with Bridget.
13) We see England from our house.
14) We are swimming.

Lesson Eight

1) Tá na fir ard.
2) Is múinteoir é.
3) Ní fir iad.
4) Tá na fir ró-ghearr.
5) Tá úlla dearga.
6) Is mé an t-innealtóir.
7) Is Éireannach tú.
8) Is é an múinteoir é.
9) Is mise an dalta.
10) Is rúnaí é an duine.
11) Is mac é an buachaill.
12) Ní seanathair é an fear.
13) Is é Seán an t-innealtóir.
14) Is í Bríd an garda.

Lesson Nine

1) D'ith mé arán agus feoil.
2) Bhí tú ag tiomáint do rothar ar an bóthar.
3) Níor d'ól muid bainne.
4) Scríobh Séamus leabhar san teach.
5) An bhfaca tú mo chapall?
6) Chuala mé na cait.
7) Dúirt Bríd le Séamus agus Máire.
8) D'oibrigh an múinteoir san scoil.

James was a teacher and he worked in the school. James did not like boys or girls, but he was good with young people. He read books with the students.

Mary: Did you talk with John about his dog?
Bridget: I didn't.
Mary: You must talk with him. I don't like his dog.

Séamus: Chuaigh tú go dtí an bhialann le Bríd. Ar ith tú feoil?
Seán: Ní d'ith mé, ach ól mé bainne agus uisce.
Séamus: An raibh Bríd sásta lena bia?
Seán: Bhí sí; ba mhaith léi a bia.
Séamus: Ar ith sí feoil nó glasraí?
Seán: Ní d'ith sí glasraí nó feoil - ith sí arán.

Lesson Ten

1) Ith/ithigí do bhia!
2) Ól/ólaigí an bainne!
3) Súil/súiligí an madra!
4) Ceannaigh/ceannaigí roinnt éadaí dó!
5) Ná abair/abraigí leis an garda!
6) Ná tar/tagaigí abhaile le Séamus!
7) Snamh/snamhaigí leis an capall!
8) Tabhair/tugaigí roinnt toradh don mhúinteoir!

John: Did you buy milk?
Bridget: I didn't buy milk, but I have water.
John: I don't like water! Buy milk for me!

Lesson Eleven

1) Íosfaidh mé mo bhia.
2) Ceannóidh tú feoil dom.
3) Ní rithfidh siad ar an mbóthar.
4) An dtiomáineoidh sí a carr?
5) Íocfaidh muid do.
6) An dtiocfaidh tú liom?
7) An dtroidfidh sé leis?
8) Beidh sibh ciúin.

Made in United States
North Haven, CT
01 January 2025